Exploring Science

The Exploring Science series is designed to familiarize young students with science topics taught in grades 4–9. The topics in each book are divided into knowledge and understanding sections, followed by exploration by means of simple projects or experiments. The topics are also sequenced from easiest to more complex, and should be worked through until the correct level of attainment for the age and ability of the student is reached. Carefully planned Test Yourself questions at the end of each topic allow the student to gain a sense of achievement on mastering the subject.

EXPLORING
ELECTRICITY

Ed Catherall

STECK-VAUGHN
LIBRARY
Austin, Texas

Exploring Science

Electricity
Light
Magnets
Soil and Rocks
Sound
Weather

Cover illustrations:
Above left Electricity pylons.
Below left A circuit diagram, showing a battery, two
bulbs, and a switch.
Right An electric light bulb.

Frontispiece A powerpoint for recharging special
batteries. The two red lights on the unit show that the
recharger is working. Four batteries are in position.

Editor: Elizabeth Spiers
Editor, American Edition: Susan Wilson
Series Designer: Ross George

**Published in the United States in 1990 by Steck–Vaughn Co.,
Austin, Texas,** a subsidiary of National Education Corporation.

First published in 1989 by
Wayland (Publishers) Ltd

©Copyright 1989 Wayland (Publishers) Ltd

Library of Congress Cataloging-in-Publication Data

Catherall, Ed.
    Exploring electricity / Ed Catherall.
        p.   cm. — (Exploring science)
    Includes bibliographical references.
    Summary: Introduces basic principles of electricity and includes
related projects and activities.
    ISBN 0-8114-2594-0
    1. Electricity—Juvenile literature.   2. Electricity—Experiments-
-Juvenile literature.   [1. Electricity.   2. Electricity-Experiments.
3. Experiments.]   I. Title.   II. Series: Catherall, Ed.   Exploring
science.   69-26117
QC527.2.C383   1990   CIP
637—dc20   AC

Typeset by Multifacit Graphics
Printed in Italy by G. Canale of C.S.p.A., Turin
Bound in the United States by Lake Book, Melrose Park, IL
        3   4   5   6   7   8   9   0   Ca   94

Contents

STATIC ELECTRICITY

Left *Spectacular static electricity sparks, made when a steel ball is dropped into a high-energy electric field.*

A Van der Graaf generator. It can produce static electricity for experiments. The surface of the shiny metal hood collects the static charges.

When you undress, you can sometimes hear a crackling sound coming from your clothes. This is best heard if you are wearing nylon next to wool. If you undress in the dark, it is possible to see tiny sparks, like lightning, coming from your clothes. The sparks from your clothes are caused by static electricity and are best seen on dry days. You can sometimes feel the effect if you walk on thick nylon carpet and then touch a metal doorknob. You can feel an "electric shock."

The Ancient Greeks noticed that amber beads rubbing against fur or wool would attract dust and hair. The Greek word for amber is *elektron*, which is where the word electricity comes from.

In the 1700s, Benjamin Franklin realized that static electricity is made of two static charges: he called them negative and positive. Negative charges are attracted to positive charges and try to reach them. When you hear your clothes crackling, your movements are rubbing the wool against the nylon, causing the nylon to be negatively charged. The wool becomes positively charged. When you separate your clothes, the nylon's negative charges jump toward the wool. You can think of these charges as "lightning sparks."

ACTIVITY

1 Tear the newspaper into very small pieces and put them on a table.
2 Bring each item close to the paper. Does anything happen?

3 Rub the pen many times with the woolen cloth.

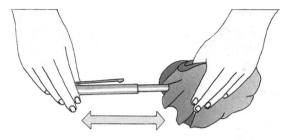

4 Bring the pen close to the paper. What happens now? Is the pen charged with static electricity?
5 Rub the plastic spoon with fur.
6 Bring the spoon close to the paper. What happens?
7 Comb your hair with the plastic comb. Is the comb charged?

8 Try rubbing the nail, the wooden ruler, and the piece of rubber with the woolen cloth. Do these become charged with static electricity?
9 Try testing other materials.
10 Which material is easiest to charge?
11 Think of an experiment that would prove this. Remember to make a fair test.

TEST YOURSELF

1. Where does electricity get its name?
2. Describe how you would put a static charge on something.
3. Why do you sometimes hear a crackling sound when you undress?

HOW IS STATIC ELECTRICITY MADE?

Everything in the universe is made of atoms. You are made of atoms; so are your table and chairs, the food that you eat, and the air that you breathe. Each atom is so tiny that it takes millions of them to form just one head of a pin.

Each atom contains charged particles. In the middle of each atom are the positively charged particles called protons, and the uncharged particles called neutrons. Around the outside of each atom move the negatively charged particles called electrons like the planets orbit the sun. You can think of the protons and neutrons as the sun and the electrons as the planets.

Before an atom becomes charged with static electricity, the number of protons equals the number of electrons, so the atom is not charged. When wool and plastic are rubbed together, electrons can be made to move from one item to the other. The atoms in the plastic pick up the electrons from the atoms in the wool. There are now extra electrons on the plastic, so it is no longer "balanced" but negatively charged. The wool has lost electrons so it too is no longer "balanced"; the protons make it positively charged. The wool and the plastic will attract each other. This is because unlike charges attract.

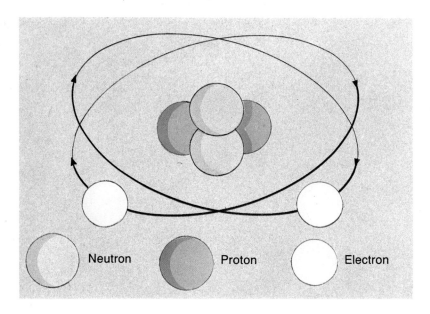

Neutron   Proton   Electron

Left *A diagram of an atom, showing the electrons, protons, and neutrons.*

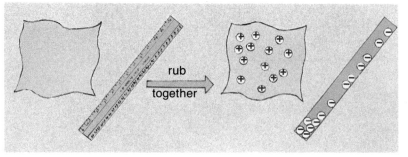

rub together

Left *A diagram to show how static charge builds up when plastic and wool are rubbed together. The plastic takes electrons from the wool, leaving the plastic with a negative charge and the wool with a positive charge.*

ACTIVITY

STATIC CHARGES

> **YOU NEED**
>
> - **a balloon inflator**
> - **a rubber balloon**
> - **thread**
> - **woolen cloth**

1 Use the inflator to blow up the balloon.
2 Tie the neck of the balloon with thread.
3 Hold the balloon by the thread and ask your friend to rub the balloon gently with the woolen cloth. Do not rub too hard or fast or the balloon will burst.

4 What happens when you bring a cloth close to the balloon?

5 Hold the charged balloon close to your friend's hair. What happens?

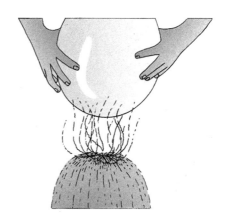

6 Place the balloon close to your nose. What can you feel?
7 Can you get a charged balloon to stick to the wall or under a table?
8 Hold your balloon above some dust or chalk dust. What happens?
9 Turn on a water tap until the water comes out as a thin stream.
10 Hold the charged balloon near it. What happens?

TEST YOURSELF

1. Is an electron positively or negatively charged?
2. Draw an atom. Label the protons and electrons.
3. What happens to the electrons when you rub a rubber balloon with a woolen cloth?

LIGHTNING

You know that static electricity makes sparks when it jumps. Perhaps the most spectacular example of this is lightning. Sometimes, particularly if it is hot, heavy clouds become charged with static electricity. Positive charges tend to collect at the top of the cloud, while negative charges move to the bottom. Eventually, the charge builds up so much that the negative electrons jump in an attempt to "balance" themselves. When they jump, or discharge, the air gets very hot. This causes the flash and also makes a shock wave of pressure, which we hear as thunder.

There are two common types of lightning. Sheet lightning is where the charge leaps from one side of the cloud to another. Forked lightning is where the charge leaps to earth, sometimes branching out to other clouds on the way down.

These cloudbanks are producing sheet lightning (above) and forked lightning (below).

Forked lightning is very dangerous. It usually strikes the tallest object, such as a tree. If you are caught in a thunderstorm, never stand under a tall tree or under a tree standing alone. Do not stand on high ground. It is quite safe inside a car or a building. Tall buildings usually have lightning rods. These are strips of metal that take the static electricity safely down the outside of the building to the ground.

Thunder, which is caused by lightning, is not dangerous. It can be used to find out roughly how far away the storm is. Sound travels much slower than light. So you hear the thunder after you see the lightning. If there is a five-second gap between them, the storm is about 1 mile away.

ACTIVITY

POSITIVE AND NEGATIVE CHARGES

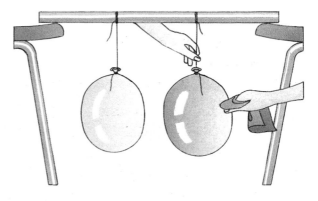

YOU NEED

- **2 rubber balloons**
- **a balloon inflator**
- **a broom handle suspended between 2 chairs**
- **thread**
- **2 empty plastic bottles**
- **a woolen cloth**

1 Use the inflator to blow up a balloon. Tie the neck of the balloon with thread.
2 Hang it from the broom handle.
3 Blow up a second balloon and hang it near the first.

4 Rub one balloon with the woolen cloth to charge it. How do the balloons react to each other?

5 Rub both balloons with the woolen cloth. You now have two negatively charged balloons. What happens?
6 Do like charges (i.e., the same charge) attract or repel?
7 Lay 2 empty plastic bottles on a table and steady them.
8 Put them close together. What happens?

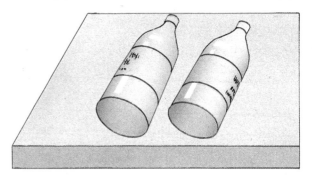

9 Rub one bottle with the woolen cloth. Place it near the other bottle. What happens?
10 Now rub both bottles with the woolen cloth.
11 What happens when the bottles are close together on the table?

TEST YOURSELF

1. What is lightning and what causes it?
2. Why do you hear thunder after you see a lightning flash?
3. Which places should you avoid during a thunderstorm?

DETECTING STATIC CHARGES

You have learned that like charges repel each other and unlike charges attract each other (see page 11). So it is easy to test whether a material is charged by bringing it close to another charged material.

An instrument that detects static charge in this way is called an electroscope. There are all kinds of electroscopes which contain different materials as the charge indicator. One of the most popular is the gold-leaf electroscope. This has two charged strips of gold. When a like charge comes near, the leaves fly apart as they repel each other. If an unlike (opposite) charge comes near, the leaves move closer together. This is because the charge on the gold leaf and the charge from the material are in balance.

It is best to use all types of electroscopes in dry air. If it is a moist day, the extra electrons can leave negatively charged material and jump onto water particles in the air. Much of the charge leaks away. Thus dry days are best for detecting static charges.

The two diagrams below show a gold-leaf electroscope: first, being approached by a rod carrying the same charge as the electroscope, and second, when the rod carries a different charge.

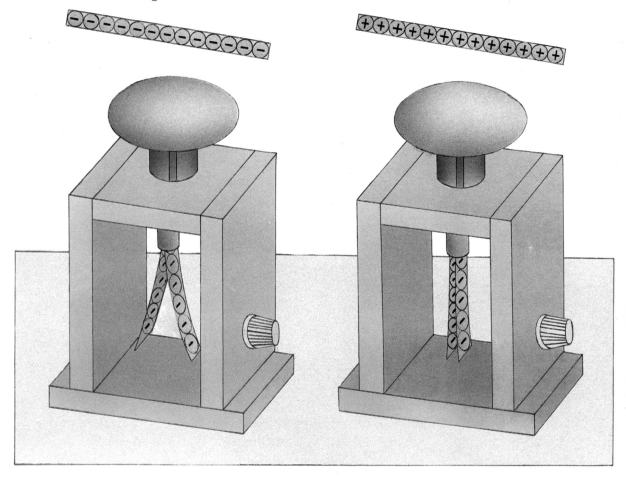

ACTIVITIES

MAKING A PAPER ELECTROSCOPE

YOU NEED

- **a long, thin strip of newspaper (10 in. × 2 in.)**
- **a woolen cloth**
- **a wooden ruler**
- **a plastic pen**
- **a plastic comb**

1 Fold the paper in half lengthwise.
2 Open it out and place it on a table.

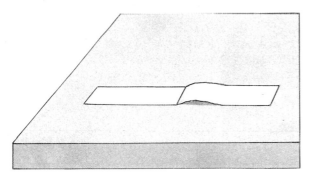

3 Stroke the paper with the woolen cloth.

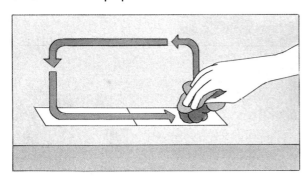

4 Pick up the paper with a ruler so that it hangs down over the ruler. What happens to the paper?

5 Rub the pen with the cloth. Hold the charged pen between the paper halves. What happens?

6 Are the charges on the paper and pen like or unlike?
7 Charge the comb. Hold it between the paper. What happens?
8 Are the charges like or unlike?

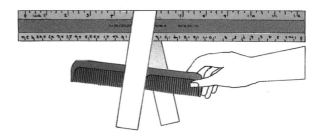

TEST YOURSELF

1. What is a static electricity detector called?
2. Why should you not attempt static experiments in damp weather?

ELECTRICITY IN YOUR HOME

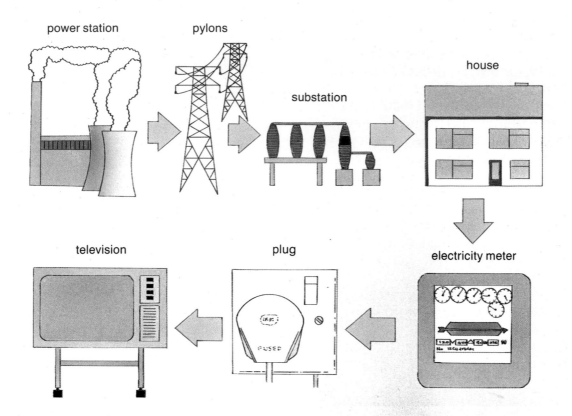

power station — pylons — substation — house — electricity meter — plug — television

Static means to stay still. Static electricity charges stay still on a material. The charges can only move if they build up too high, such as in a thunderstorm. They jump away from the material; this is called a discharge.

Electricity is not always static, or staying still. In some substances, such as metal, the electrons (negative charges) can flow. This is called current electricity. We can use wires to channel the electricity into machines to do work.

Power stations create the current electricity that flows along wires until it reaches our homes. Before the electricity is used in the home, it flows through a meter which records how much is used.

Electricity is a form of energy. Thus it can

This is the pathway of electricity that we use in our homes, places of work, and in industry. Electricity is made in the power station and passes through a number of stages before it is used.

be changed into other types of energy. A great deal of the current electricity used in the home is changed into heat energy. The flowing electrons may be used to heat the element in an electric range, an iron, or a heating system. Electrical energy also may be converted to light energy in a light bulb, or to sound energy in a radio or a television speaker. Mechanical (movement) energy can be made from the current and used to turn motors in a dishwasher, washing machine, or electric drill.

ACTIVITY

READING THE METER

1 Ask someone where your electric meter is.
2 Look at it. It will be one of two kinds: new-style, digital display or old-style, dial meter.
3 The new-style, digital display has a set of numbers. This is the meter reading. It will change as electricity is used in your home.

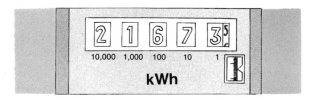

4 The old-style, dial meter is easy to read once you know how. There should be five dials.
5 Read the dials from left to right. There are examples to help you.

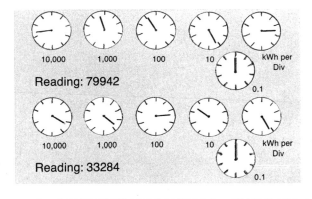

Reading: 79942

Reading: 33284

6 For either type of meter, look to find the wheel that turns when there is current flowing somewhere in your home. You will see only part of it.

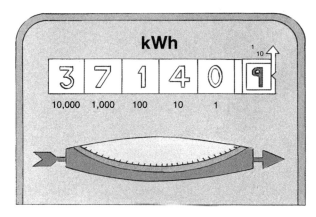

7 If possible, ask an adult to switch on different types of electrical equipment: something that heats up, gives sound, gives light, has a motor. Watch the wheel.
8 What type of electrical equipment makes the wheel turn fastest? This costs the most to use.
9 Look at the meter reading every day. How much has it changed?
10 Do this for several days.
11 Find out how much electricity your house uses each day. Is it roughly the same each day?
12 Are some days more expensive than others? If so, can you think of reasons why?

TEST YOURSELF

1. What is the difference between static and current electricity?
2. Name three electrical appliances that convert electrical energy into heat energy.
3. Name three electrical appliances that convert electrical energy into mechanical energy.

DRY-CELL BATTERIES

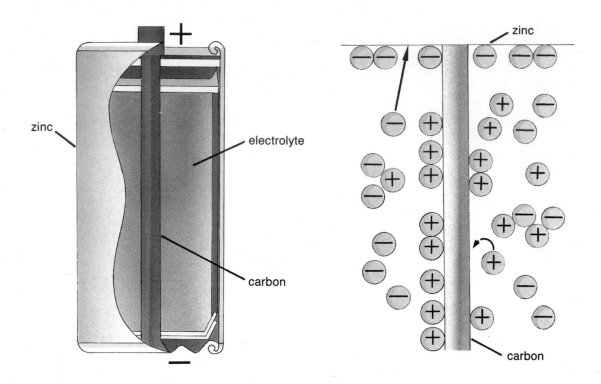

Two diagrams of a dry-cell battery. The diagram on the left shows the contents of the battery. At right, how the charges move to make an electric current.

You do not always use the household current to power equipment in your home. It is very strong electricity, which can be inconvenient for small appliances, such as radios. It is also very dangerous. The shock from touching a bare wire might kill you. The best device to use in small pieces of equipment, and for electrical investigations like the ones in this book, is a dry-cell battery. You may have used these in flashlights, calculators, and radios.

A battery turns chemical energy into electricity. Dry-cell batteries are not really dry, but contain a damp, chemical paste called electrolyte. This is made up of millions of positive and negative charges. The electrolyte is put into a battery case made of zinc. In the middle of the battery is a carbon rod, which often has a metal tip for

a good connection to the equipment. The carbon rod and the zinc case are the electrodes of the battery. They are connected to the "+" and "−" terminals outside the battery.

When a dry cell placed inside a flashlight is switched on, a chemical reaction starts in the paste. Electrons go to the zinc case and positive charges go to the carbon rod. The flow of electrons that goes into the flashlight's wires makes the bulb light up. When the electrolyte cannot make any more electrons, the battery is dead and no more current will flow.

ACTIVITIES

3 If they are covered in thick paper, remove the paper to see the zinc case. What do you notice about the case?

YOU NEED

- **a selection of used dry-cell batteries**

1 Look at the shapes of the batteries. What do they have written on them?
2 What are their voltages? Where are the terminals?

WARNING: DO NOT OPEN THE BATTERY. The electrolyte could burn your eyes, skin, and clothing. (Inside the battery is only a black carbon rod and some dark gray paste. It is not worth the risk or the effort of looking inside!)

MAKE YOUR OWN WEAK BATTERY

2 Tightly wind one end of a piece of wire around the paper clip.
3 Stick the paper clip into the lemon.

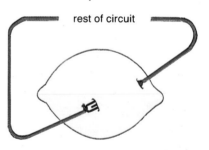

YOU NEED

- **2 short pieces of insulated copper wire**
- **a large paper clip**
- **a large, juicy lemon**
- **a 1.5V bulb in a bulb holder**

6 Push the other terminal of the second wire deep into the lemon.

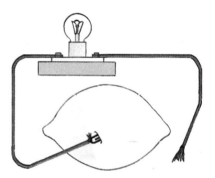

rest of circuit

1 Uncover the ends of the wire.

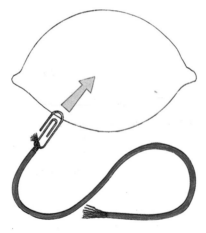

4 Attach the other end of the wire to the bulb holder.
5 Attach the other piece of wire to the other terminal of the bulb holder.

7 Darken the room. Does the bulb glow?
8 Jiggle the wires in the lemon.

TEST YOURSELF

1. Explain why you must never play with household electricity.
2. Draw a dry-cell battery. Label the parts.

CIRCUITS

On page 17, you turned a lemon into a dry-cell battery. To prove that you made electricity, you used your battery to light a bulb. In a dry-cell battery, the electrons within the electrolyte cannot move until there is a pathway linking the zinc to the carbon electrode.

If you connect the zinc electrode to a bulb with a wire, then run another wire from the bulb to the carbon electrode, there is a path for the electrons to flow through. This path is called a circuit.

There are a lot of electrons at the zinc electrode (negative) and much fewer at the carbon terminal (positive). Unlike charges attract, so if there is a circuit for the electrons to flow along, they will move from negative to positive. To keep the flow going, the battery uses an electrical force called the voltage. This is the difference in charge between the two electrodes and is measured in volts (V), named after Alessandro Volta, an Italian scientist who made the first electric cell, or battery.

The current is measured in ampères or amps (A), named after the French scientist A.M. Ampère.

A microscope photograph of a set of microchips (integrated circuits). These are tiny, complicated circuits containing many parts, found in many electrical devices, including computers. The microchip circuits are printed on a wafer made of silicon.

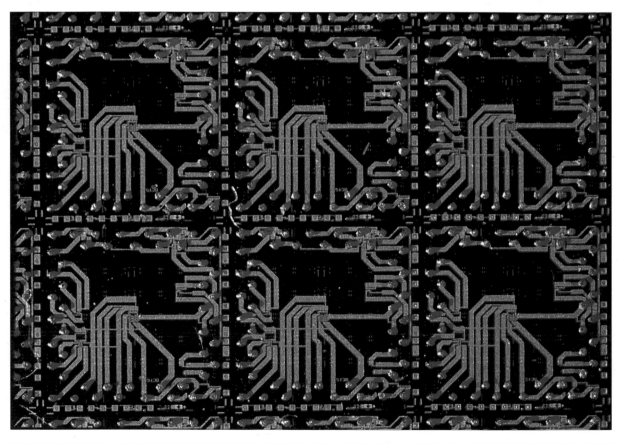

ACTIVITY

MAKING A SIMPLE CIRCUIT

YOU NEED

- **a screwdriver**
- **2 short lengths of insulated copper wire**
- **2 crocodile terminal clips**
- **a bulb in a bulb holder**
- **a dry-cell battery in a battery holder**

---

1 Check that the ends of the copper wires are uncovered.
2 Connect one crocodile clip to one end of a length of wire.
3 Connect the other end to one side of the bulb holder.
4 Fasten the crocodile clip to one battery terminal.

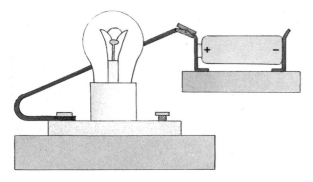

5 Notice that the bulb does not light up, as there is no circuit (pathway) for the electrons.

6 Now connect another clip to the second wire, and the free wire's end to the other side of the bulb holder.
7 Fasten this crocodile clip to the other battery terminal.

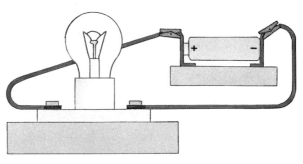

8 What happens? If the electrons can flow around the circuit from the zinc to the carbon the bulb should light.
9 Disconnect one crocodile clip from the battery terminal.
10 What happens to the bulb? Why?
11 Swap the terminals. Does the battery still work?

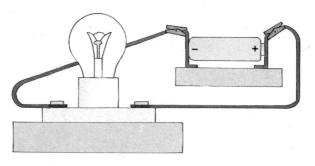

12 Draw your complete circuit showing the bulb lit.

WARNING: Do not leave the bulb on for long. You will waste both bulb and battery.

TEST YOURSELF

1. Why is a circuit necessary for electricity to flow?
2. Draw a simple circuit.
3. What is the difference between volts and amps?

SERIES CIRCUITS

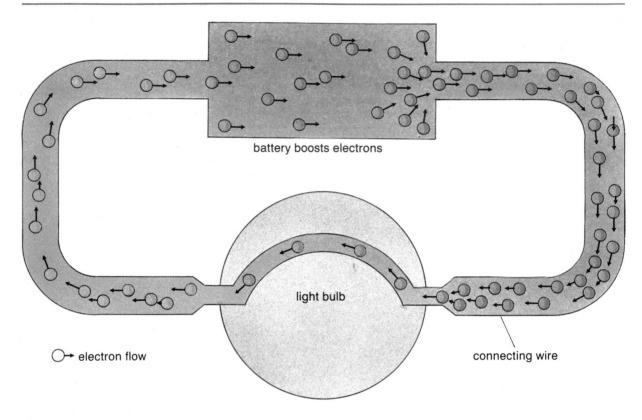

battery boosts electrons

light bulb

○→ electron flow

connecting wire

When an electric circuit is made, electrons flow from the negative terminal of the battery to the positive terminal. In order to see that the electric current is flowing a bulb can be put in the circuit. Electrical energy becomes light energy in the bulb.

A bulb is rather like a narrow bridge. The electrons are slowed down as they jostle to cross the bridge. This means that they have less energy to complete the circuit, where they are boosted again by the battery. We could put a second bulb in the circuit after the first bulb in a series. This is called a series circuit. The electrodes now have two bridges to cross. They have twice the work to do. There are not enough electrons crossing both bridges to light both bulbs strongly, so the bulbs are dimmer than before.

Electron flow in a circuit containing a battery and a light bulb. The wire in the light is like a narrow bridge. The electrons lose energy as they cross this bridge.

You can now add a third bulb in series. The electrons have to pass through three lamps, so they are dimmer still. More electrons could be added by adding more batteries to the circuit. The batteries must be connected positive to negative terminal to complete the circuit. Now the bulbs have more electrons and should be brighter.

Remember: electrons need a complete circuit to flow. Any break in the circuit will prevent the flow of electricity and the bulbs will go out. If a bulb is removed from a series circuit, the other bulbs will fail. Christmas tree lights often work in series.

ACTIVITY

MAKING A SERIES CIRCUIT

YOU NEED

- **a screwdriver**
- **6 short lengths of insulated copper wire**
- **2 dry cell batteries in battery holders**
- **a switch**
- **3 bulbs in bulb holders**

1 Connect a wire from one positive battery terminal to one side of the switch. Connect another wire from the switch to the bulb holder.

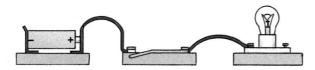

2 Connect the third wire from the bulb holder to the negative battery terminal. You have made a circuit.

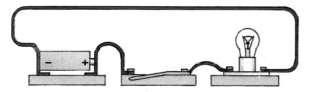

3 Switch on. Does the bulb light? If not, check your circuit.

4 Connect another bulb holder to the circuit.

5 Switch on. Do both bulbs light?

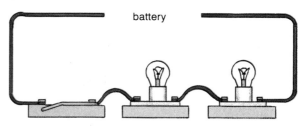

6 Is each bulb as bright as when there was only one bulb in the circuit?

7 Put a third bulb in the circuit. Switch on. What happens?

8 Unscrew one bulb. Switch on. What happens? Why?

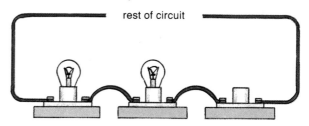

9 Put a second battery into the circuit. Remember to connect the positive terminal of one battery to the negative terminal of the other battery.

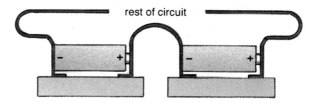

10 Switch on. Are the bulbs bright now?

TEST YOURSELF

1. How does a switch turn off electricity?
2. Why do bulbs glow more dimly when you add more of them to a series circuit?
3. Draw a series circuit with 2 batteries and 2 bulbs in it.

PARALLEL CIRCUITS

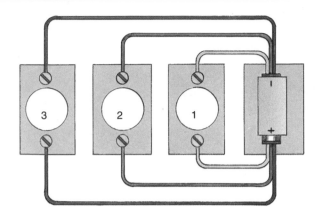

In a series circuit, the light bulbs are placed in a series one after the other, like beads in a necklace. The electrons in the circuit have to pass through each bulb before returning to the positive electrode of the battery. If a bulb breaks or fails, the circuit is broken and all the bulbs fail.

However, there is a way to wire a circuit full of bulbs so that one can fail while the other bulbs stay lit.

Suppose that you want to wire three bulbs. Bulb 1 is wired to the positive and negative terminals of a battery. So is bulb 2, in its own little circuit. The same goes for bulb 3. This system of wiring is called a parallel circuit, because each simple circuit is parallel to another. An electron has a choice of little simple circuits to travel through. If it passes down circuit 1, it will light bulb 1, and so on. The current divides equally between all three circuits. If one bulb fails, it only breaks one of the

simple circuits and that bulb goes out. The other two circuits are still intact and their pathways complete. The other two bulbs will stay lit. It is therefore easy to identify the broken bulb in a parallel circuit. To identify a broken bulb in a series circuit, each bulb must be tested in turn.

Attaching more bulbs in parallel to a battery will not dim the bulbs. Each gets the battery's force and lights up brightly.

The national Christmas tree in Washington, D.C. The lights are arranged in parallel circuits, so if one light bulb fails, the others in the display will stay lit.

ACTIVITY

MAKING A PARALLEL CIRCUIT

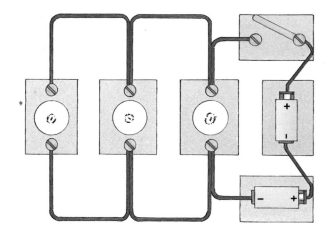

> **YOU NEED**
>
> - **3 bulbs in bulb holders**
> - **a screwdriver**
> - **7 short lengths of covered copper wire**
> - **2 batteries and holders**
> - **a switch**

7 Connect the two batteries. Switch on. Do all the bulbs light?

8 Unscrew one bulb and remove it. Switch on.

1 Put three bulb holders side by side.

2 Connect together one side of all the bulb holders, using two wires.

3 Use another two wires to connect the other side of the bulb holders.

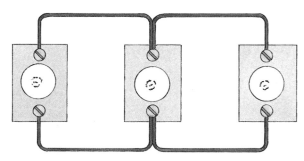

4 Run a wire from a positive battery terminal to one side of the switch.

5 Run another wire from the switch to one side of the first bulb holder.

6 Connect the other side of the first bulb holder to the negative battery terminal.

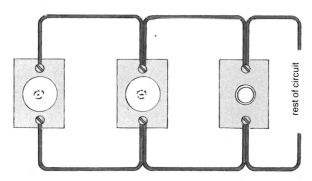

9 Do the other two bulbs light? What happens to their brightness?

10 Follow the pathway of the electrons from the negative battery terminal around your parallel circuit.

11 Switch off.

12 What happens when you unscrew another bulb?

TEST YOURSELF

1. What is an advantage of a parallel electric circuit compared to a series electric circuit?

2. Draw a diagram of a parallel electric circuit that uses a battery, a switch, and three bulbs.

3. Describe how a parallel circuit works.

CONDUCTORS AND INSULATORS

These wires are insulated with poor conductors so they do not pass electricity to one another.

Electrical energy is in one way like heat energy: it travels better through some materials than through others. Where it travels easily, the material is called a good conductor. Metals are good conductors of electricity. These materials contain electrons that can move about more easily than in bad conductors. Normally, electrons move in the conductor randomly.

If you connect one end of a good conductor to the negative terminal of a battery and the other end to an electric circuit, electricity will flow along the conductor. You have made a pathway for the electrons to flow from the negative terminal of the battery to the positive terminal. The differ-ence in the number of electrons at one end compared to the other end is called the potential difference. This is measured in volts.

A bad conductor is called an insulator. An insulator has few mobile electrons. When an insulator is connected to a battery, not enough electrons in the insulator can move to give an electric current. As no current is formed, no electricity passes.

Insulators, therefore, act as a barrier to electricity. Copper is a good conductor; rubber is a good insulator. Electrons stay in copper wire covered with rubber and go around the circuit. The rubber stops the electrons from "leaking" away.

ACTIVITY

MAKING A CONDUCTIVITY BOARD

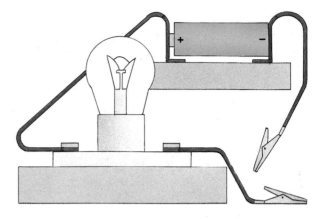

YOU NEED

- **a screwdriver**
- **3 short lengths of insulated wire**
- **a battery**
- **a bulb and bulb holder**
- **2 crocodile clips**
- **objects to be tested, made of plastic, glass, rubber, and wood; include a copper wire, iron nail, brass screw, pencil**

1 Connect one wire to the negative battery terminal and the two other wires to either side of the bulb holder.

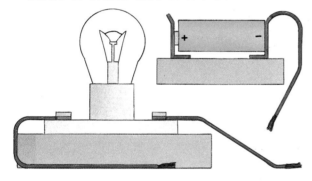

2 Connect one side of the bulb holder to the positive battery terminal.

3 Connect a crocodile clip to both free ends of wire.

4 Connect the two ends of the copper wire with the crocodile clips. What happens?

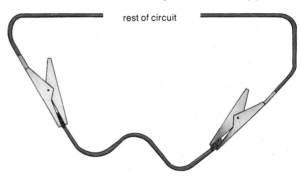

rest of circuit

5 Notice that the copper wire conducts electricity, completing the circuit. The copper is therefore a good conductor. Record your result.

6 Fix the plastic between the clips. Is the plastic conducting electricity? If not, plastic is an insulator.

7 Try all kinds of materials to see if they are conductors or insulators. Record your results.

8 Sharpen both ends of a pencil. Is pencil "lead" a good conductor?

TEST YOURSELF

1. What is the potential difference in a circuit?
2. Explain how a good conductor conducts electricity in an electrical circuit.
3. Describe how you could test a material to see whether it is a conductor or an insulator.

ELECTRICAL RESISTANCE

Good conductors of electricity have many mobile electrons. Thus electrons from a battery easily pass through a good conductor. As they move, they collide with atoms and slow down. This slowing down of the electrons is called the resistance of the conductor.

All conducting wires have a resistance, as they are all made of atoms that the electrons can collide with. The longer the piece of wire, the more atoms there are for the electrons to bump into and be slowed down by. So, the longer the wire, the higher its resistance. That is why, in experiments using circuits, we try to use short wires to cut down resistance.

Thick wire has a lower resistance than thin wire. In thick wire, there is a wider area for the electrons to pass through. Thus there is more room for the electrons to avoid collision with atoms. So thin wire has a greater resistance than thick wire.

We measure resistance in ohms, named after the German scientist, Georg Simon Ohm, who worked on resistance in the nineteenth century. He stated "Ohm's Law," which says that the resistance (R) of an electrical circuit is the number of volts in the circuit (V) divided by the current (I), measured in amps:

$$R = V \div (I)$$

Same thickness but different length:

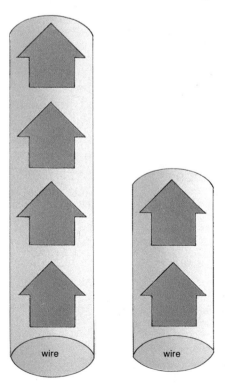

Same length but different thickness:

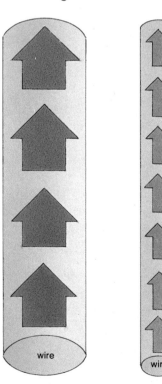

ACTIVITY

VARIABLE RESISTORS

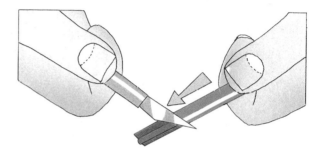

YOU NEED

- **a collection of pencils of differing hardness**
- **a battery**
- **a bulb and bulb holder**
- **a screwdriver**
- **5 short lengths of insulated wire**
- **a small saw**
- **a sharp knife**

WARNING: Be very careful when using a saw or a knife.

1 Set up the circuit as on page 25.

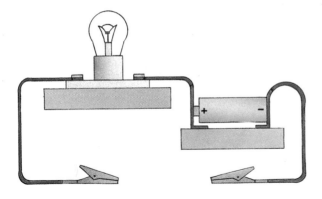

2 Use the saw to cut the pencils to the same length.
3 Carefully cut away all the wood from one side of the pencil until you have exposed the pencil "lead."

4 Notice that the darkest pencil "lead" is the softest.
5 Soft pencil "leads" are almost all graphite. To harden it, graphite is mixed with clay. Graphite is a form of carbon that conducts electricity.
6 Test the conductivity of each pencil.

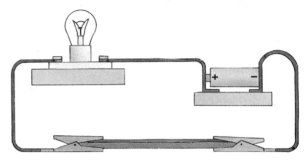

7 Compare the brightness of the bulb to the pencil hardness.
8 You should find that the harder the pencil, the higher its resistance.
9 Bring the clips closer together while touching the pencil "lead." What happens to the light?

Variable resistors control the amount of electricity passing through them. Variable resistors are used as light dimmers and volume controls on radio and television.

TEST YOURSELF

1. What is the difference between hard and soft pencils?
2. What does a resistor do in an electrical circuit?
3. Name two uses for a variable resistor.

HEAT FROM ELECTRICITY

This electric bar heater has coils of wire with a naturally high resistance.

One of the main uses of electrical energy is to convert it into heat energy. We use this in electric heaters, dryers, irons, and ranges. Remember how fast these appliances made the wheel on the electricity meter spin?

All of these devices work because of electrical resistance. When electrons pass down a wire, they collide with atoms. The more atoms with which they collide, the greater the resistance. When the electrons collide with the atoms, they make the atoms vibrate. These vibrating atoms are hit by more electrons, causing them to vibrate more and more, causing the material to get hotter and hotter. In order to get the maximum number of collisions, we first use a wire that has a naturally high resistance, such as nickel-chrome wire. We then make

this wire very thin. Thin wire increases the resistance because it acts as a narrow bridge to the passage of the electrons, thus increasing collisions.

If we are not careful, the hot wire will weaken, so we usually wrap it around a china-like substance that will heat up and give out heat as well.

Obviously, the more electric power provided, the more electrons there are to collide with the atoms to generate heat. We measure this electric power in watts (W), named after James Watt, who invented the steam engine. In electricity, watts are volts multiplied by amps:

$$P = V \times (I)$$

Most electric heaters are measured in kilowatts, or 1000 watts.

ACTIVITY

HEAT FROM ELECTRIC POWER

YOU NEED

- a screwdriver
- 3 lengths of insulated copper wire
- a battery
- a switch
- a bulb in a bulb holder
- a styrofoam cup with a small amount of water
- cellophane tape
- thermometer

1 Connect together the battery, switch, and bulb.

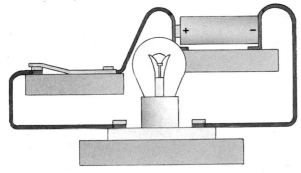

2 Check that the bulb and circuit work.
3 Place the bulb in the styrofoam cup, so that the glass of the bulb is underwater.
4 *Make sure that only the glass of the bulb is in the water.*

5 Tape the wires to the cup to hold the bulb in place.

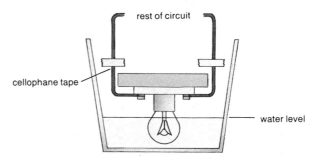

6 Use the thermometer to test the temperature of the water.
7 Record this temperature.
8 Switch on and leave the light on in the water for five minutes.

Temperature of water before switching on (°F)	
Temperature of water after 5 minutes (°F)	
Temperature of water after 10 minutes (°F)	

9 Record the temperature of the water. How much has the temperature increased?
10 What happens if you leave the light on for ten minutes?
11 What happens if you use two bulbs?

Remember: For the best results, you need the smallest amount of water.

TEST YOURSELF

1. Name three pieces of equipment that convert electrical energy into heat energy.
2. Explain how an electric heater works.
3. How do we calculate the electrical power of a heating appliance such as an electric heater?

LIGHT FROM ELECTRICITY

If you look at any electric light bulb, you will see that the filament that glows is very thin. This filament is similar to the element in an electric heater. The filament is a fine coil of wire that has a high resistance. The wire is usually made of tungsten, because tungsten can get white-hot and still not melt. Tungsten wire has a high resistance.

In order for the tungsten wire to glow white-hot, it must be very long and very thin. To get this long length of wire into a light bulb, the wire is coiled in a tight coil and then loosely coiled again. The wire

coil is long, thin, and heavy, so stronger wires support it inside the bulb.

If the bulb were full of air, oxygen in the air would combine with the tungsten. When the tungsten got hot, it would burn up instantly. For this reason, all air is taken out of the bulb and the bulb is refilled with a harmless, inactive gas called argon.

Like the electric heater, the power of the light bulb is written on the glass bulb. The power is measured in watts (see page 28). Most household bulbs are 40 W (dimmest), 60 W, 75 W, 100 W or 150 W (brightest).

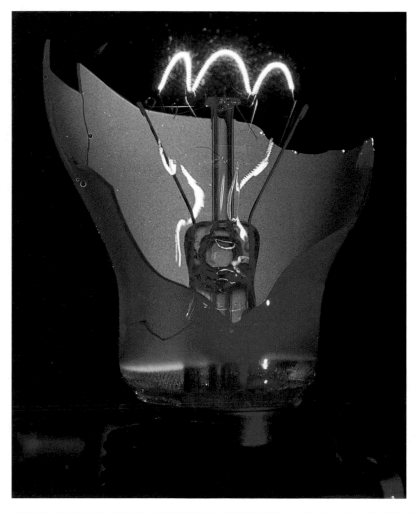

This is an ordinary household bulb. The filament, or fine wire coil, is made of a metal called tungsten, which has a high resistance. It is very thin, and glows as it is heated up by the efforts of the electrons to pass through it.

ACTIVITY

LOOKING AT BULBS

> **YOU NEED**
>
> - **a collection of light bulbs, including floodlight bulbs and various clear household bulbs**
> - **a magnifying lens**

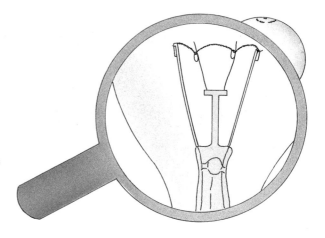

1 Look at a clear light bulb. What wattage is this bulb? What does this tell you?

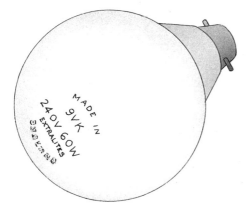

2 How does the bulb fit into its lamp socket?

3 Look at the fitting end of the bulb. What is it made of? Where does the electricity enter the bulb?

4 Notice how the electric wires are separated by the glass stem.

5 Look through a lens at the coils and loops in the tungsten coil.

6 Notice how it is supported and can move gently within the supports.

7 Will this bulb work or not? Look at the coil. Is it intact or broken?

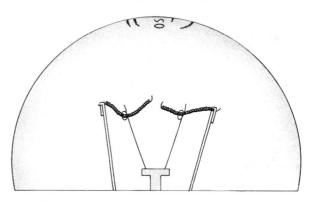

8 Compare this bulb with other household light bulbs. Draw what you see. Label the parts.

9 How does a common light bulb differ from a floodlight bulb?

10 Draw a floodlight bulb.

11 Arrange your bulbs in order of brightness. How can you do this without testing them?

TEST YOURSELF

1. What is the wire in a light bulb made of?

2. Why is a light bulb full of argon gas?

3. Explain how electric power is turned into light power.

FUSES

The dry-cell batteries that we use give less than one amp of electricity and are very safe. Household electricity is much more powerful, and thus can be dangerous.

If too much current flows into an appliance, the electrons could "leak away" in large numbers. If you come into contact with current leaks, you could be killed by an electric shock. In addition, the appliance could catch fire, or be ruined in some other way. To prevent this from happening, each circuit in the house, and every appliance, has a control to regulate the amount of electricity going through it. These controls are called fuses.

A fuse works by resistance. If the correct amount of electricity passes in the circuit, the fuse acts as a wire, allowing the circuit to work. If too much electricity passes, due to a fault in the wire or an appliance, the fuse heats up because it is a resistor. It heats up quickly and melts, breaking the circuit. No more electricity will pass until the fault is repaired. If you do not repair the fault, but just replace the fuse, this new fuse will also melt, breaking the circuit again.

The type of fuse that you may have seen is probably a cartridge. Inside the glass case of the cartridge is the fuse wire. Fuses are of different sizes, depending on the amount of electricity they will allow to pass before melting.

Cartridge fuses used in a car.

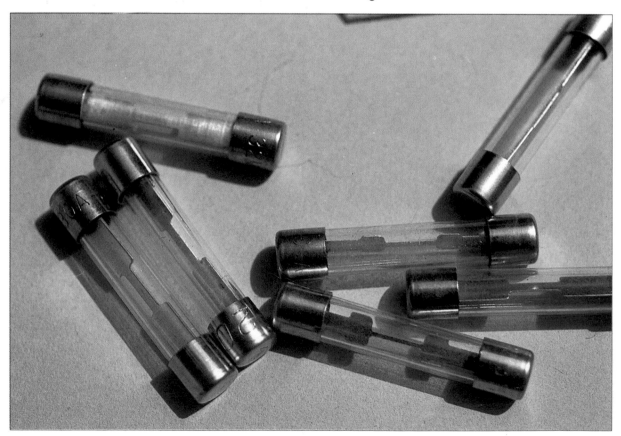

ACTIVITY

YOU NEED

- **a screwdriver**
- **3 short lengths of insulated copper wire**
- **2 crocodile clips**
- **a battery**
- **a switch**
- **steel wool**
- **a wood block**
- **a collection of cartridge fuses**
- **a magnifying lens**

1 Use the insulated wire to connect one clip to one battery terminal.
2 Use another length of wire to connect the other battery terminal to one side of the switch.
3 Connect the other side of the switch to a clip.

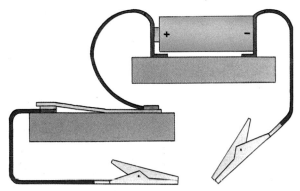

4 Separate your steel wool. Select one strand.

5 Put this strand of steel wool onto the wood block.
6 Check that the switch is off.
7 Use clips to grip each end of the strand of steel wool.

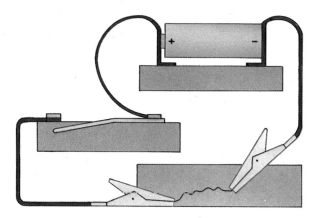

8 Switch on. What happens to the steel wool?
9 Use two batteries if you have trouble with your steel wool fuse.
10 Do not do this experiment too many times as it drains the battery.
11 Look at your collection of fuses through a magnifying lens.
12 Look at a 3 amp, 5 amp, and 13 amp fuse. Why are the wires different thicknesses?
13 Are all of the fuses intact or have some burned out?

WARNING: This experiment could be dangerous. Get an adult to help you.

TEST YOURSELF

1. What does a fuse do?
2. Why should you always use the correct fuse, as specified on the appliance?
3. Explain how a fuse works.

WATER CONDUCTS ELECTRICITY

Electrolysis (destroying by electricity) of a metal in a conducting solution, such as salt water. This is part of an electrical circuit, which will work only if the metal is dipped into the solution. The electricity breaks down the water, producing bubbles of hydrogen, which is one of the elements that make up water. The metal gradually dissolves as more electricity passes.

To be able to conduct electricity, a material must be a good conductor (see page 24). A good conductor has many mobile electrons.

Pure water does not have any mobile electrons to form an electric current. Thus pure water is an insulator. Table salt is a chemical called sodium chloride. When sodium chloride dissolves in water it ionizes. That means that it splits into ions, which are electrically charged particles. There are sodium ions (positive) and chloride ions (negative) in the water. The word ion comes from a Greek word meaning wanderer which describes the way in which these ions move freely in the water. The ions also make water break down into ions.

The chloride ions with their negative charges can act just like electrons and carry electricity through the water. The more ions in the water, the more charges there are present, so more electricity can flow. Most water has some chemicals dissolved in it. All dissolved chemicals ionize. Tap water has chemicals dissolved in it, so it conducts electricity. Because of this, never use any electrical appliance near water. Never touch an electrical plug, or any electrical appliance, with wet hands or the electricity will go through you, giving an electric shock that could kill. Your hands can also conduct electricity if they are sweaty, because sweat contains salt.

ACTIVITY

YOU NEED

- **a screwdriver**
- **3 short lengths of covered copper wire**
- **a battery**
- **a bulb in a bulb holder**
- **a jar**
- **pure (distilled) water**
- **tap water**
- **a spoon**
- **salt**

1 Connect one battery terminal to one side of the bulb holder.
2 Run a wire from the other side of the bulb holder into the empty jar.
3 Connect a wire to the other battery terminal and put that wire in the jar.

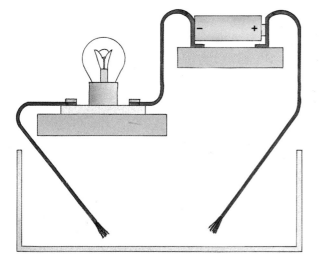

4 Touch together the wires in the jar.
5 You have now made a circuit and the bulb should light.
6 Separate the wires in the jar. The bulb will go out.
7 Half fill the jar with distilled water.
8 Check that the ends of the wires are covered by the water.

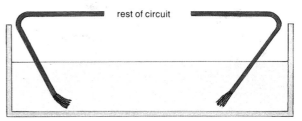

rest of circuit

9 Does the bulb light? Is electricity passing through the water? Is pure water an insulator or a conductor?
10 Empty out the pure water.
11 Replace it with tap water. Does the bulb light?
12 Bring the wires closer together. What happens?
13 Stir some salt into the water. Does salt water conduct electricity?

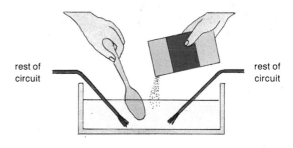

rest of circuit   rest of circuit

14 Slowly move the wires apart. What happens?
15 What happens with more salt?

TEST YOURSELF

1. Is pure, distilled water a conductor or an insulator? Why?
2. What happens to salt when it is dissolved in water?
3. Why must you never touch electrical appliances with wet hands?

ELECTROPLATING

Steel is a strong metal that is used to make many things. Unfortunately, steel rusts. You can prevent rusting by coating the steel. You can paint the steel or coat parts of it with chromium. When the steel on cars is covered with chromium we use the term chrome plated, which means electroplated with chromium.

Expensive spoons are made of silver and hallmarked to show this. Some spoons have E.P.N.S. stamped on them. This means electroplated nickel silver. Here, the spoon is electroplated with silver. It has only a fine coat of silver on it, although it looks like a silver spoon.

To electroplate a spoon with silver, the chemical silver nitrate must be dissolved in water. In water, silver nitrate splits into silver ions (positive) and nitrate ions (negative). A spoon is then connected to the negative terminal of the battery and so becomes the negative electrode, which we call the cathode. A bar of silver is attached to the positive terminal of the battery and becomes the positive electrode, or anode. As the electric current passes, the positive silver ions in the water are attracted to the negative (cathode) spoon and stick to it. The negative nitrate ions are attached to the positive electrode, which is the bar of silver. The nitrate ions cause the silver on the bar to dissolve, making more silver ions. This goes on until the spoon is smoothly plated with silver. You will notice that the silver bar is used up in this process.

Electroplating a nickel spoon. The silver anode dissolves to form silver ions, which move to the nickel cathode and become silver metal again.

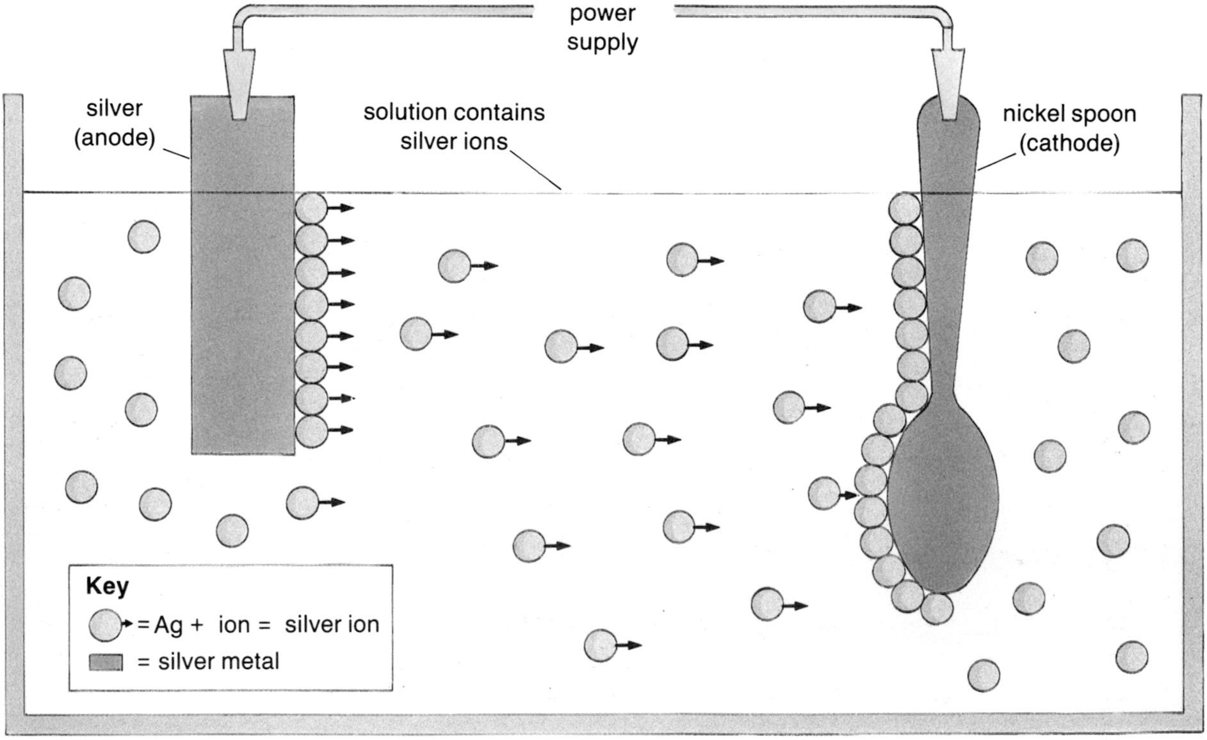
power supply
silver (anode)
solution contains silver ions
nickel spoon (cathode)
Key
= Ag + ion = silver ion
= silver metal

ACTIVITY

ELECTROPLATING WITH COPPER

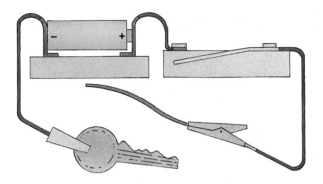

YOU NEED
- **an empty milk carton**
- **a bottle of white vinegar**
- **salt**
- **an object to be plated such as a brass key**
- **a battery**
- **3 short lengths of insulated wire**
- **2 crocodile clips**
- **a switch**
- **a bar of copper**
- **cellophane tape**

1 Cut a clean milk carton in half.
2 Half fill the carton with white vinegar.
3 Stir salt into the vinegar until no more will dissolve.

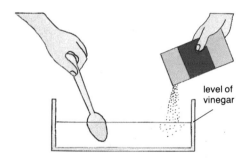

level of vinegar

4 Connect the brass key to be plated to the negative battery terminal, using a crocodile clip and wire.
5 Connect the positive battery terminal to a switch.

6 Connect the switch to the copper, using a crocodile clip and a wire.
7 Place the copper bar and key in the tank until they are mostly covered by vinegar. Keep the clips dry.
8 Tape the wires to the side of the carton with cellophane tape.

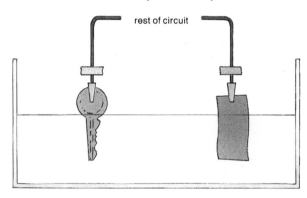

rest of circuit

9 Switch on. What changes do you notice on the key?
10 Are bubbles being formed? If bubbles stick to the key, shake them off.
11 How long does it take for the key to be covered in copper?
12 Look at the copper bar. What is happening to it?

TEST YOURSELF

1. What is a negative electrode called? What is a positive electrode called?
2. When silver nitrate ionizes in water, which is the positive ion?
3. Describe how you could electroplate a spoon.

STORING ELECTRICITY

Left *A spark plug from a car showing the electric arc (spark) that must be made at regular intervals for the car to run smoothly.*

Below *A diagram of a lead-acid battery (accumulator), used in cars.*

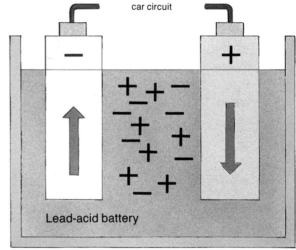

car circuit

Lead-acid battery

Cars, when they are moving, use most of their energy to generate electricity. Cars do this by using an alternator, which is similar to a dynamo (see page 44). Cars need electricity to power the lights and other electrical parts of the car. Cars also need to store electricity so that there is power to start the car.

The car battery is an accumulator (storer of electrical energy) as well as a battery (provider of electrical energy). Car batteries are often lead-acid cell batteries. The first lead-acid cell batteries were invented in 1881, and were important in the development of the first cars.

A lead-acid cell battery consists of a series of cells. Each cell consists of plates of lead immersed in dilute acid. When the engine is running, electricity passes to the lead-acid cells for storing. There are lead plates at the positive and negative terminals acting as electrodes. Some lead cells are cathodes and some are anodes. The positive plate (the anode) becomes coated with lead oxide. The negative plate (the cathode) stays as lead.

When the engine is switched off, no more lead oxide forms and the electrical energy is stored. The car needs electrical energy to start, and when the ignition key is turned, the lead oxide on the anode starts to combine with the acid to form lead sulfate and water. This continues until no lead oxide is left and the battery is "dead." When the battery is recharged with electricity, the lead sulfate is turned back to lead oxide and acid, and electricity is stored.

ACTIVITY

STORING ELECTRICITY IN A LEAD-ACID CELL

YOU NEED

- **sodium sulfate (Glauber's salt)**
- **a glass jar**
- **2 small strips of lead**
- **2 short lengths of insulated copper wire**
- **cellophane tape**
- **a screwdriver**
- **2 good, strong, dry-cell batteries (6V)**
- **a bulb and bulb holder**

1 Dissolve sodium sulfate in warm water to make a strong solution.
2 Half fill the jar with the solution.
3 Attach each strip of lead to a length of covered copper wire. Make sure there is a good connection. Tape the wires to the lead.

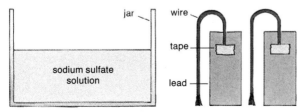

4 Connect the other end of the wires, one to the positive terminal of one battery, the other to the negative terminal of the other battery.

5 Join the batteries in series.
6 Put both strips of lead into the sodium sulfate solution. Do not let the lead strips touch.

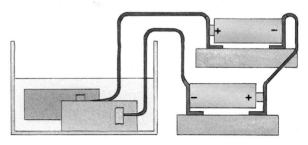

7 What happens to your storage cell?
8 Do bubbles appear on the lead?
9 Does the positive lead strip, the anode, change color?
10 After five minutes, your lead-acid cell should be charged.
11 Disconnect both batteries.
12 Carefully connect the wires from your storage cell to a bulb in a bulb

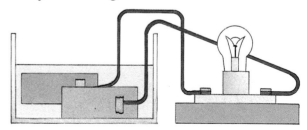

holder. Does your bulb light?
13 Notice how your storage cell soon becomes drained.

TEST YOURSELF

1. What does a car battery do?
2. Explain what happens when electricity is fed into a lead-acid cell.
3. Explain what happens when a lead-acid cell acts as a battery to provide electricity.

ELECTRICITY MAKES MAGNETISM

When electrons flow through a wire and make an electric current, a magnetic field is created around the wire. This magnetic field, or magnetism, is created as a magnetic force spiraling around the wire. Magnetism is created clockwise about the wire, in the direction of the electric current.

A magnetic compass needle usually points north because the magnetized needle of the compass is attracted to the earth's magnetic north pole. If a magnetized compass needle is placed near a copper wire the compass needle will continue to point north, because copper is not a magnetic metal and so will not affect the compass needle. But if the copper wire is carrying an electric current, the magnetic field that is made will immediately affect the compass needle. The direction of the flow of electricity will determine whether the magnetic field created near the magnetized compass needle is north or south. If it is a south field, the compass needle will be strongly attracted. If it is a north field, the needle will be strongly repelled.

The strength of the magnetic field depends on the number of electrons flowing through the wire. Therefore, the more electricity flowing through the wire, the greater the magnetic field around the wire.

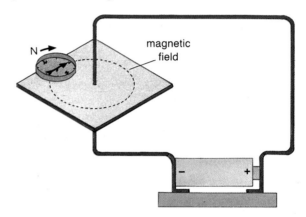

Below *A small magnet hovers above a piece of superconductor. The electricity in the superconductor creates a magnetic field, which repels the other magnet.*

Above *A diagram to show the effect of a wire carrying electricity on a magnetic compass. The electricity in the wire creates a magnetic field around it.*

ACTIVITY

YOU NEED
- **a screwdriver**
- **a length of insulated copper wire**
- **a 6V battery**
- **a switch**
- **a bulb in a bulb holder**
- **a magnetic compass**
- **a small cardboard or plastic box**

1 Make a circuit using the battery, switch, and bulb holder. Switch on.
2 Does the bulb light? Switch off.
3 Place the compass on the wire. Check that the compass needle points north.
4 Move the wire so that it also points north-south, in line with the needle.

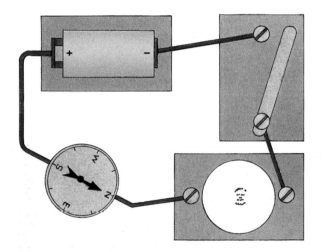

5 Switch on. Does the bulb light? What happens to the compass needle when electricity flows through the wire?
6 Switch off. What happens?
7 Try this with the battery connected the other way around.

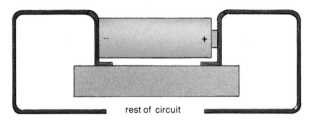

rest of circuit

8 Place the compass in the box.
9 Wind the copper wire 10 times around the box.

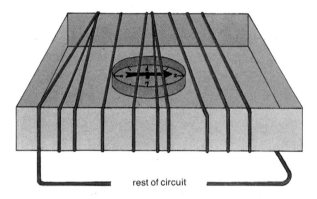

rest of circuit

10 Switch on. Does the compass needle move more than before?
11 Wind the copper wire 20 times around the box. Does the compass needle react even more?
12 Does the number of turns of wire increase the magnetic effect?

TEST YOURSELF

1. Describe how you would prove that a magnetic field is created when electrons flow through a wire.
2. When electricity flows through a wire where is the magnetic field created?
3. Explain how the number of turns in a coil of wire affects the amount of magnetism created.

ELECTRIC MOTORS

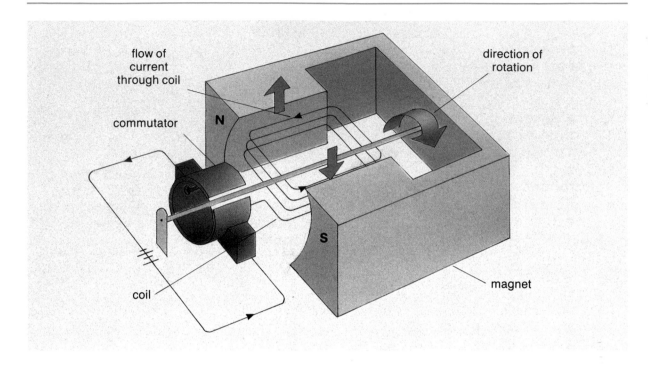

A diagram to show the main parts of a simple electric motor.

You have learned that electricity and magnetism are closely linked and can have an effect on one another. Electric motors use this relationship to turn electrical energy into mechanical (movement) energy.

An electric motor consists of a coil of wire held in a magnetic field made by a permanent magnet. A flow of electrons (current) is sent through the coil. The magnet affects the moving electrons and makes the coil turn. This is because the current makes a magnetic field around the wire. The current is sent through the wire in such a way that to start with, the north pole of the magnet lines up with the north pole of the magnetic field around the wire. The two poles repel each other, and this causes the coil to turn toward the unlike pole of the permanent magnet.

Just before the coil lines up north-south with the magnet and gets fixed in position, the flow of electricity is sent the other way. Now the north pole of the coil has become its south pole (see page 40). By the time the poles of the coil switch, like poles of the coil and permanent magnet are again lined up. The poles again repel each other and the coil continues to turn.

Once again, just before the unlike poles line up, the current is reversed. This continues, and the coil keeps on turning. The spinning coil can be used to turn other components attached to the motor.

The current that changes direction every half-turn is called an alternating current (a.c.). Household current is alternating. If the current comes from a battery and only flows in one direction (direct current or d.c.), the motor has a special attachment inside it called a commutator, which reverses the current when necessary.

ACTIVITY

YOU NEED

- **a screwdriver**
- **4 short lengths of insulated copper wire**
- **an electric motor and the battery that powers it**
- **a switch**
- **a crocodile clip**
- **a sharp knife**
- **a new pencil**

1 Make a circuit by connecting together the battery, switch, and motor. Switch on.
2 Does the electric motor turn?

3 Disconnect your circuit.
4 Fasten a crocodile clip to one end of a length of insulated wire.
5 Connect the other end to the negative battery terminal.
6 Connect one wire from the positive battery terminal to one side of the switch.
7 Connect the other side of the switch to one side of the motor.
8 Connect a wire to the other side of the motor.
9 Use a crocodile clip to grip this wire. Switch on.

10 Is your circuit complete? Does the motor turn? Switch off.
11 Sharpen one end of the pencil. Using the knife, carefully cut away all the wood from one side of the pencil to expose the whole lead.
12 Use the crocodile clip to grip the sharpened end of the pencil. Switch on.
13 Touch the loose wire to the middle of the pencil lead. Does the motor turn?
14 You control the motor by

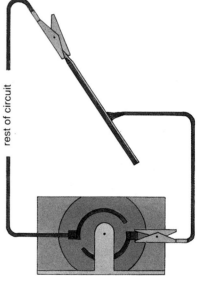

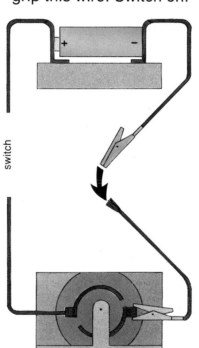

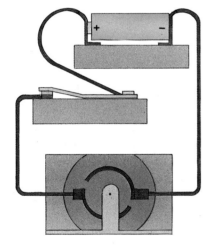

moving this wire along the lead.
15 When it turns slowly, try to see how the electricity flow is reversed in the coil.

TEST YOURSELF

1. Name three things that use an electric motor.
2. Why is magnetism important for an electric motor to work?
3. Describe how an electric motor works.

GENERATING ELECTRICITY

Electricity will drive an electric motor. The motor converts electrical energy into mechanical energy. If mechanical energy is used to turn a coil inside a magnetic field, electricity is made. An electric motor used to create electricity in this way is called a dynamo. The generator in a power station is a dynamo. First, you need power to turn the dynamo. Sometimes, falling water (as in hydroelectric power) or steam power is used. When steam is used, burning fuel or nuclear power heats the water and creates steam. The steam or the falling water turns the blades of a turbine, thus driving the dynamo. A transformer increases the voltage of the electricity produced.

The electricity produced in the United States is at 230,000 volts and travels along wires strung between great pylons. This electricity is alternating current (a.c.). A dry-cell battery produces direct current (d.c.). It only flows in one direction. Alternating current changes direction 120 times a second, called 60 cycles. Sending electricity as alternating current at this high voltage means that there is less power loss due to heat. This can happen when the electricity is sent over great distances. Of course, these wires need massive insulators. This electricity is too powerful for our homes, so it is reduced by transformers in substations to 120 volts, or in some places to 220 volts. The power of household current varies in different countries. In the United States the current is reduced to 120 volts. In Europe it is reduced to 240 volts.

Electricity may be delivered to our homes in one of two ways. It may come through underground cables or it may come through overhead wires.

Very thick insulating material is used to isolate the cables that carry electricity at very high voltages across the country. Without such isolators, the cables would pass their electricity to one another, and cause widespread power cuts.

ACTIVITIES

RESEARCH INTO ELECTRIC POWER GENERATORS

> **YOU NEED** • **access to a library**

1 Look up steam electrical generators.
2 Look at cost and safety. What are the advantages of generating steam using coal, oil, or nuclear power? What are the disadvantages?

3 Find out about hydroelectric power, wind power, solar power, wave and tide power, and other alternative energy sources.
4 Mount a display of this research.

MAKING ELECTRICITY

> **YOU NEED**
>
> • **a magnetic compass**
> • **a cardboard or plastic box**
> • **a long length of fine covered wire**
> • **a broom handle**
> • **a strong bar magnet**

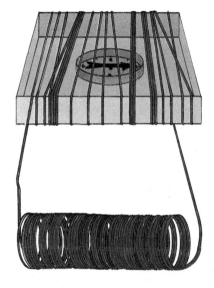

1 Put the compass in the box.
2 Wind 20 turns of wire around the box.
3 Pass the wire's other end around a broom handle 50 times to make a coil.

4 Check that the coil is far enough from the compass.
5 Slowly put the north pole of your bar magnet into the 50-turn coil. What happens to the compass needle?

6 If the needle moves there must be electricity in the wire. Slowly withdraw the magnet. What happens?
7 Slowly put the south pole of the magnet into the coil. What does the direction of the needle tell you?
8 How could you make a stronger electric current in the coil?

TEST YOURSELF

1. Name three ways that an electrical generating power station is fueled.
2. Why is electricity sent across country at such a high voltage?
3. What is a dynamo and how does it work?

Glossary

Alternating current (a.c.)   An electric current that flows first in one direction, then in the opposite. The direction changes at regular intervals.

Appliance   A piece of equipment that is powered by electricity.

Attraction   In electricity, the power or force that pulls two unlike charges together. In magnetism, the power or force that pulls two unlike poles together.

Carbon   An element found in all living things, as well as in graphite, diamond, and coal.

Conductor   In electricity, a substance through which electrons flow easily. Very good conductors have a low electrical resistance.

Current   The flow of electrons through a conductor. It is measured in amperes (amps).

Direct current (d.c.)   An electric current that flows in one direction only.

Electrode   A conductor through which electric current enters or leaves a battery or electrolyte.

Electrolyte   Usually a solution or liquid that conducts electricity. However, electrolytes do have other forms: for example, a pastelike substance inside dry-cell batteries. The difference between an electrolyte and a conductor, such as a metal, is that the electrolyte contains ions to carry the charge. In a conductor, electrons move.

Electron   A negatively charged particle present in all atoms. Free electrons are responsible for electrical conduction in most materials.

Electroplating   A method of coating one metal with another, usually by passing an electric current through a special circuit. The metal to be coated acts as one electrode and the metal for coating acts as the other electrode, with the conducting solution between the two.

Filament   A very thin thread.

Insulator   A material that is a very bad conductor, e.g., plastic, rubber, wood.

Mobile   Easily able to move or be moved.

Ohm   The unit used to measure electrical resistance.

Potential difference   The difference in electrical force between two terminals.

Power   The rate at which work is done, or energy is used. Electrical power is measured in watts.

Proton   A positively charged particle that is found in the nucleus of every atom. Its charge exactly balances that of one electron.

Pylon   In electricity, a tall, steel tower that carries electrical wires.

Repel   To push away from. In electricity, the effect of two like charges on each other. In magnetism, the effect of two like poles on each other (repulsion).

Resistance   In electricity, the ability of a substance to conduct electricity. The higher the resistance, the less current passes through. It is measured in ohms.

Transformer   A device that alters the voltage of an electric current, either increasing or decreasing it.

Turbine   A revolving motor in which a wheel with blades is driven by a liquid or gas passing through it.

Voltage   Electrical force. It is measured in volts.

Wattage   Electrical power. It is measured in watts.

Books to Read

How Did We Find Out About Electricity?
Isaac Asimov (Walker & Co., 1973)
The Light Bulb: Inventions That Changed Our Lives, Sharon Cosner (Walker & Co., 1984)
Electricity: From Faraday to Solar Generators, Martin Gutnik (Franklin Watts, 1986)
Wires & Watts: Understanding and Using Electricity, Hal Keith (Scribner, 1981)
More Wires & Watts: Understanding & Using Electricity, Hal Keith (Scribner, 1988)

Picture Acknowledgments

The author and publishers would like to thank the following for allowing illustrations to be reproduced in this book: PHOTRI 32; Science Photo Library 6, 18, 24, 30, 38, 40; Topham Picture Library 28; ZEFA *cover*, 8, 22, 34, 44. All artwork is by Marilyn Clay. Cover artwork by Jenny Hughes.

Index